Healthy Dogs, Your Loving Touch Series

Healthy Dogs - Soothing Massage
The Effleurage Technique Made Easy

Off The Leash Press, LLC

www.OffTheLeashPress.com

Healthy Dogs, Your Loving Touch Series

Healthy Dogs - Soothing Massage
The Effleurage Technique Made Easy

Sherri Cappabianca, CSAMP, CSAAP

Certified Small Animal Massage Practitioner
Certified Small Animal Acupressure Practitioner
www.RockysRetreat.com

Off The Leash Press, LLC

www.OffTheLeashPress.com

The information presented here is for the purpose of helping dog owners learn effleurage massage, a skill used as a complement to regular veterinary care. Effleurage massage is not intended as a substitute to regular veterinary care, nor is this book intended to offer any advice, diagnosis or treatment. Please consult with your veterinarian for any symptoms requiring diagnosis and possible treatment.

Published by:
Off The Leash Press, LLC   www.offtheleashpress.com
PO Box 275   info@offtheleashpress.com
Winter Park, FL 32790-0275   **407-758-8309**

First Edition

Editing and consultation services: Rik Feeney
Cover design: Sherri Cappabianca
Front cover photograph: photopix|iStockphoto.com
Rear cover photograph: happyborder|iStockphoto.com

All interior photographs by Dana Brooks, with the exception of:
- p. iii ©Temele|Dreamstime.com
- pp. viii, 17, 21, 22, 23, 80 ©Sherri Cappabianca
- p. 12 ©sonyae|iStockphoto.com
- p. 15 ©Peterbetts|Dreamstime.com
- p. 18 © Pk-Photos|iStockphoto.com
- p. 6 ©Vencavolrab|Dreamstime.com
- p. 65 ©Paigefalk|iStockphoto.com
- p. 58 ©happyborder|iStockphoto.com
- pp. 1, 54 ©Isselee|Dreamstime.com
- pp. 2, 11 ©Darrenw|Dreamstime.com
- p. 13 ©syagci|iStockphoto.com
- p. 16 ©Radekk|iStockphoto.com
- p. 24 ©Sam Charles Hodgson
- p. 63 ©Lucyz|Dreamstime.com
- p. 68 ©rhyman007|iStockphoto.com
- p. 74 ©stanfair|iStockphoto.com

Library of Congress Control Number: 2010907285

LIBRARY OF CONGRESS CATALOGING-IN-PUBLICATION DATA
Cappabianca, Sherri
Healthy Dogs - Soothing Massage: The Effleurage Technique Made Easy / by Sherri Cappabianca.
ISBN: 978-0-9841982-1-4

1. Dogs-Health. 2. Dogs-Diseases-Alternative treatment. 3. Massage for Animals.
4. Complementary Care. I. Title

Contents

Dedicated with love to my four-legged boys,
Rocky and Yankee.
Rocky was my inspiration, and is still missed today.
Yankee is our joy, full of life and love.

CHAPTER ONE
How is Your Dog?

For dog lovers everywhere, there's nothing more heartbreaking than to watch your dog, your faithful companion get old, lose his vibrancy and youth, and then pass away. Most of us would do ANYTHING, spending ANY amount of money to help our beloved friends stay healthy and live longer.

Since we all want our beloved companions to remain healthy and vibrant for as long as possible, the question ultimately becomes "What can I do to help my dog live longer and healthier, and be happier, so I have the most quality time with him I can have?" The answer is often found in complementary and alternative care such as massage.

So, how is your dog? Does he have arthritis? Is he a senior? Does he not like to be touched? Is he an abused rescue? Does he have behavior quirks or health issues? Or, do you have a puppy and want him to get used to being handled, to make sure he learns to trust you and stays physically and emotionally healthy? What about a working

1

or service dog, an amateur athlete, or a dog that likes to have fun? Any of these questions, as well as many others, can be addressed with the massage stroke known as "effleurage." Effleurage is a gentle, yet powerful and versatile stroke that can be used for a complete massage.

> *Complementary and alternative therapies were **never** meant to replace regular veterinary care. If you suspect something is wrong with your dog, **always** consult with your veterinarian first.*

I remember a special time when I worked on an old Labrador Retriever. She was so old she could hardly move, but she was still alert, eating, and drinking, and happy. Her owners weren't ready for her to pass on, and from what I could tell, neither was she. Her owners asked me to do massage on her, since they understood the importance of keeping the circulation and fluids moving through her body. She was very thin, and had almost no muscle tone left. The only stroke I could do on her was effleurage. She wasn't able to handle the deeper or more vigorous strokes. But that was OK, effleurage was all she needed. I worked on her regularly and taught her owners how to work on her as well. They did, in between my visits. With each subsequent visit, I could see a change in this old gal. She seemed to have more pep, she could get up a bit, and she had more spark and sparkle in her eyes. She did pass away, but I believe (and her owners do too) the regular effleurage massage not only prolonged her life but gave her a better quality of life during the time she had left.

What are Some Benefits of Massage for Dogs?

While the benefits massage on dogs are numerous and varied, here are a few of the more important ones:

- lessens behavioral issues, decreases fear, anxiety and stress, calms nervous temperaments, and relieves emotional pain (such as separation anxiety),

- builds trust,

- increases the acceptance of touch, especially to paws, which also fosters socialization and trust development,

- maintains and improves overall and long term health,

- soothes tired or tense muscles and relieves aches and pains,

- increases circulation,

- strengthens the immune system,

- aides athletic ability and works to improve the performance of your show, service, or competition dog,

- speeds recovery from surgery, injury or illness,

- strengthens the body and enhances muscle function and tone,

- increases joint flexibility and range of motion,

- reduces swelling in the joints caused by arthritis,

- helps to maintain a shiny coat and healthy skin,

- delays the onset of old age; and,

- improves the quality of life for both you and your dog.

Animal massage is not the same as petting. When massaging your pet, your intention is to affect the animal's health and well-being, using deliberate, controlled, and focused strokes. Your purpose is multifold – to help heal, to increase the bond with your animal, to give back to a beloved friend, and most important, to be aware of your dog's body so changes and potential problems can be detected early.

Massaging versus Petting Your Dog

Canine Massage is not the same as petting. When massaging your pet, your intention is to affect the animal's health and well-being, using deliberate, controlled, and focused strokes. Your purpose is multifold – to help heal, to increase the bond with your animal, to give back to a beloved friend, and most importantly, to be aware of your dog's body so changes and potential problems can be detected early.

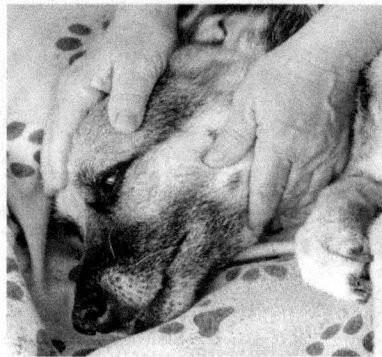

In my experience, most people want to be active and educated participants in their dog's health and well-being. That being the case, who better to give your dog a massage – why, you of course! And so it's for you this book was written. This book shows you how to use effleurage, an easy to learn yet effective stroke that will help keep your dog healthy and happy.

While massage is not a substitute for the compassionate care of your dog's veterinarian, this healing therapy can be a wonderful complement. Massage can be as important as good nutrition, companionship, and regular exercise.

CHAPTER TWO
Overview of Effleurage Massage

Have you ever had a massage? If so, I bet you felt wonderful afterward! The benefits of massage on humans are well documented, so why shouldn't the same benefits apply to dogs as well? I believe they do!

Studies show consistent massage will enhance your dog's comfort, emotional stability, general fitness, and overall health. Massage on a regular basis may add years to any dog's life and delay the onset of old age. It is an effective tool to improve the physical, emotional, and mental health of your dog. Massage is focused time with your animal, different from casual petting, and has the proven ability to reduce stress and promote a feeling of calm in both you and your dog.

What is Effleurage?

Effleurage comes from the French verb meaning "to skim" or "to touch lightly on." Effleurage is one of the principal strokes in massage, and because the stroke is so gentle, can be performed on any part of the dog's body, even over bony areas. As such, effleurage is the one stroke used most often. Rhythm, pressure, rate, and duration are the factors that make this a versatile stroke.

The effleurage stroke is so versatile an entire massage can be done using this one stroke. Effleurage is a long, smooth, flowing stroke, applied with either one or both hands, following the direction of your dog's fur. It is a soothing stroke that generally uses light pressure, and is performed with an open, flat, relaxed hand, similar to petting or stroking the fur. When using both hands the movement is hand over hand; a stroke with one hand is followed by a stroke with the other hand over the same area. With single-handed effleurage, one hand performs the stroke, while the other hand rests on the dog. Among other positive effects, effleurage warms the body, increases blood flow, and relaxes your dog.

Depending on your dog, his size, age, "job," activity level, and health, effleurage can be done with varying degrees of speed and pressure, using the fingers or thumbs, or performed with an open, flat, relaxed hand held in different ways.

What is the Purpose of Effleurage?

The effleurage stroke has a wide range of purposes, achieving specific goals depending on stroke speed and pressure, and your focus during the massage. Some of these purposes are:

- To familiarize your dog with the idea of therapeutic touch.
- To aid the elimination of waste products from the body.
- To warm the tissues.
- To help with muscle relaxation.
- To increase blood flow.

- To stimulate the peripheral nerves.

- As part of a pre-event warm up routine, to bring a generous amount of blood, oxygen, and other nutrients to the muscles.

- To drain and relax the muscles as part of a post-event cool down routine.

- To promote skin and coat health.

- To increase flexibility by breaking up tightness and restrictions in the muscles and tissues.

- To connect all parts of the body at the end of a session to complete relaxation.

When You Shouldn't Massage Your Dog

Now that you know a bit about what effleurage is and some benefits, let's discuss when you should refrain from massing your dog. There are some conditions when you should not massage your dog, or certain parts of your dog. These include but are not limited to:

- **Cancer** – massaging a dog with cancer can cause the cancer to spread. This is subject to debate and may not apply for all types of cancer, but it is better to be safe. If you want to massage a dog with cancer, please get permission from your vet.

9

- **Open wounds or abrasions** – do not massage in the area of the wound.

- **Recent fractures** – do not massage on or close to the fracture. However, you can perform a gentle massage above and below the fracture area, stroking in the direction of the heart. This increases blood flow and aids healing.

- **Acute trauma**, such as torn muscles, internal bleeding, or sprains – these conditions should be evaluated by a vet. Once healing has begun, start with light massage as long as your vet agrees and your dog is accepting.

- **Some acute nerve or spinal diseases** – massage can be too painful in these cases, or may be too painful in certain areas of the body.

- **Acute arthritis** – again, this may be too painful. Chronic arthritis should be massaged using a light touch, if your dog is accepting.

- **Fever** – a dog with a fever should be seen by a vet. Fever implies infection or other serious illness, and a massage can cause the infection to spread, or tax a system already working hard to fight the illness.

- **Shock** – this is a situation that calls for immediate veterinary care.

- **Chronic heart problems** – such as a weakened heart, can put additional stress on the circulatory system.

- **Pregnancy** – only light massage should be done, if your dog is agreeable.

- If your dog tells you he doesn't want one. Never force your dog to participate in a massage.

- If you're not in the mood. Your dog will pick up on this and neither one of you will reap the benefits.

If there is ever a doubt, ask your veterinarian!

Along with complementary care, I also want to stress taking charge of your dog's health care and looking at options that will help keep him healthy throughout his life. These options are found in food choices, exercise, mental stimulation, and companionship, in conjunction with regular, responsible veterinary care, and alternative therapies such as massage, acupressure/acupuncture, chiropractic, Reiki, aromatherapy, and herbal and homeopathic remedies. The goal is to prevent problems before they occur, leading to better health and longevity.

CHAPTER THREE
Why Effleurage?

Why would you want to do effleurage on your dog? That depends on your dog! From puppies, working or service dogs, performance or show dogs, rescues to seniors, the reasons for effleurage, the benefits, and techniques will vary. An easy to learn stroke, effleurage is ideal for most dogs.

Puppies

It's important to socialize dogs when they are puppies to ensure they are able to interact throughout their lives with various humans and other dogs. Part of socialization is to get puppies used to the idea of human touch. Becoming comfortable with human touch relaxes puppies, increases their trust in you, and makes it easier for your veterinarian and others to handle them. Effleurage facilitates this process. Physically, effleurage can ease growth stages, help with

13

blood circulation to those fast growing muscles and bones, and keep growing joints flexible.

Since most puppies have short attention spans, use effleurage in slow steady strokes for a few moments at a time. Make sure the strokes are slow and maintain even pressure. Work on different areas of the body to get your puppy used to being touched in all areas of his body. This is also a good time and way to get your puppy used to having his paws handled. This will be important as your puppy ages and needs to have nails trimmed or paws groomed.

Performance and Show Dogs

Performance and show dogs experience a heightened sense of stress and tension before a performance, and give their all during the performance. These dogs love it, but the tension and body strain exists. Therefore, it's important to warm up your dog before a performance and cool him down afterward. While the subject of canine sports massage for top canine athletes is a topic beyond the scope of this book, it's critical to ensure these dogs maintain peak health to perform their best. If your dog is a serious competitor or skilled athlete, I recommend you employ the services of a qualified sports massage practitioner to keep your dog in top physical condition.

However, if you have a dog that loves or needs organized exercise or is an amateur competitor, and you would like to try some basic warm-up and cool-down techniques with your dog, effleurage is a great choice. Before a performance, effleurage can increase circulation, warm muscles, and improve flexibility. After your dog's performance, effleurage will relax your dog, soothe and loosen tensed muscles, remove toxins that build up during intense exercise, speed recovery, and help you notice areas of possible concern, such as injury, swelling, tenderness or unusual heat.

Working or Service Dogs

Working and service dogs spend significant time "on the job" and as a result are often under some sort of stress. In time, this stress can take a toll on the dog's mind and body. Effleurage is easy to use massage technique that will help your service or working dog relax. Effleurage can also maintain or improve your dog's focus, mental function, and performance.

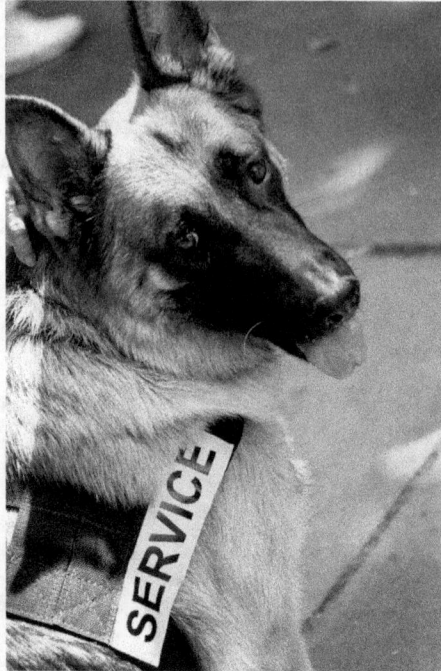

Adopted Rescue Dogs

Adopted rescue dogs often come with emotional baggage. I've known and worked with many that shy away from being touched and others that may snap at you when touched on certain parts of their bodies. Irrational fears, behavior, and other problems may also affect rescue dogs. Effleurage is a great massage technique to help these dogs overcome issues from earlier experiences. Slow, gentle, and soothing effleurage in short regular sessions can go a long way to heal the emotional problems your rescue may have, and work to forge a strong, lasting bond and trust in you.

Senior Dogs

Effleurage is an ideal massage stroke to use on senior dogs, such as dogs with arthritis, pain, limited mobility, circulation problems, or other issues related to aging. Because effleurage is such a gentle, yet effective technique, it can relieve the pain, stress, and discomfort associated with aging, while helping to increase circulation, flexibility, support for the immune system, and more.

Dogs Recovering from Surgery, Illness, or Injury

With veterinarian approval, effleurage works well to speed your dog's recovery from surgery, illness, or injury. Effleurage improves the functioning of the immune system, removes toxins from the body, increases circulation, decreases inflammation, helps to manage pain, reduces stress, and more.

All Dogs

Effleurage is a simple and effective massage technique to use on all dogs. Regular effleurage can be used to palpate your dog ("see" your dog with your hands) so you become familiar with his body. In doing so, you notice changes earlier, catching potential problems before the problem becomes serious.

Regular effleurage increases the bond with your dog, reduces stress, increases circulation, flexibility and movement, and improves overall well-being and quality of life for both of you. Consistent effleurage can enhance your dog's comfort, emotional stability, general fitness, and overall health, which may delay the onset of old age. Effleurage is an effective tool to improve the physical, emotional, and mental health of your dog.

18

CHAPTER FOUR
Canine Anatomy

W hat does your dog look like on the inside? What are those body parts we routinely rub? This chapter highlights the basics of canine anatomy, so you can visualize the dog's muscle and bone structure. Use this section as a reference to become familiar with canine anatomy. This knowledge will give you confidence to trust what your hands feel during your massage sessions.

The illustrations presented in this chapter are meant to give you a basic introduction to canine anatomy and the concepts and terms referred to within this book. The three illustrations shown are:

- **External Landmarks** – This illustration shows the common external landmarks or surface features of the dog's body. Landmarks or surface feature are used to describe the relative location of other parts of the body, such as muscles, organs, or bones.
- **Skeleton** – This illustration shows the canine skeleton from a side view and identifies the most important bone structures. Components of the skeleton serve as identification landmarks while you are working on your dog.

- **Superficial Muscles** – Another side view, this illustration shows the dog's superficial muscles only and identifies the primary muscles you will be working on during your sessions.

Once you are more familiar with canine anatomy and are regularly massaging your dog, you'll be better able to determine if something is not quite right, and can inform your veterinarian right away.

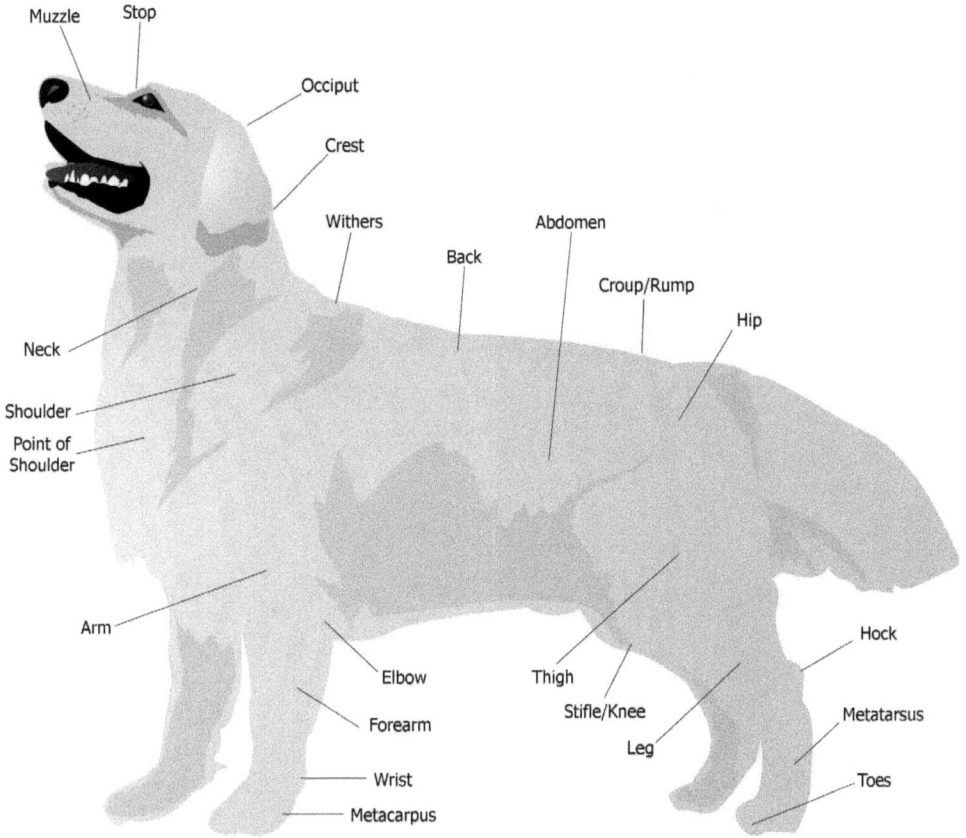

Muzzle · Stop · Occiput · Crest · Withers · Abdomen · Back · Croup/Rump · Hip · Neck · Shoulder · Point of Shoulder · Arm · Elbow · Thigh · Hock · Forearm · Stifle/Knee · Metatarsus · Leg · Wrist · Toes · Metacarpus

Canine External Features

External features are used as a reference by dog fanciers, veterinarians, and such for discussion purposes when talking about a certain part of the body. Even though dogs vary greatly in size and shape, all dogs share the same external features.

Skull

Occipital
Bone

Cervical
Vertebra

Thoracic
Vertebra

Lumbar
Vertebra

Sacrum

Mandible

Pelvis

Axis

Femur

Atlas

Scapula

Point of Shoulder

Rib

Humerus

Tibia

Fibula

Radius

Point of Hock

Ulna

Sternum

Costal cartilage

Patella

Carpals

Tarsals

Metacarpals

Metatarsals

Phalanges

Phalanges

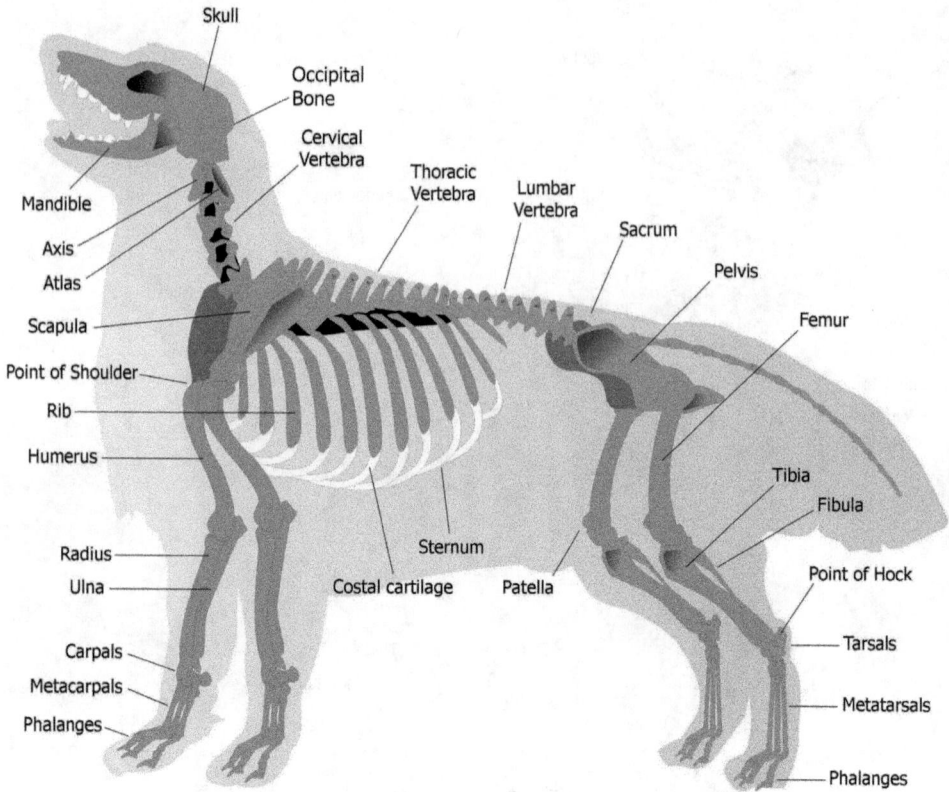

Canine Skeleton—Side View

The skeleton forms the framework of the dog's body. It gives your dog his shape, provides attachment points for musculature, works with muscles to generate movement, and encloses and protects the vital organs and soft tissues of the body.

Frontalis

Masseter

Trapezius

Sternocephalicus

Latissimus Dorsi

Middle Gluteal

Brachiocephalicus

Superficial Gluteal

Deltoid

Semitendinosus

Triceps Brachii

Sartorius

Biceps Femoris

Biceps Brachii

Digital Extensors

External Obliques

Digital Flexors

Deep Pectoral

Tensor Fasciae Latae

Digital Flexors

Digital Extensors

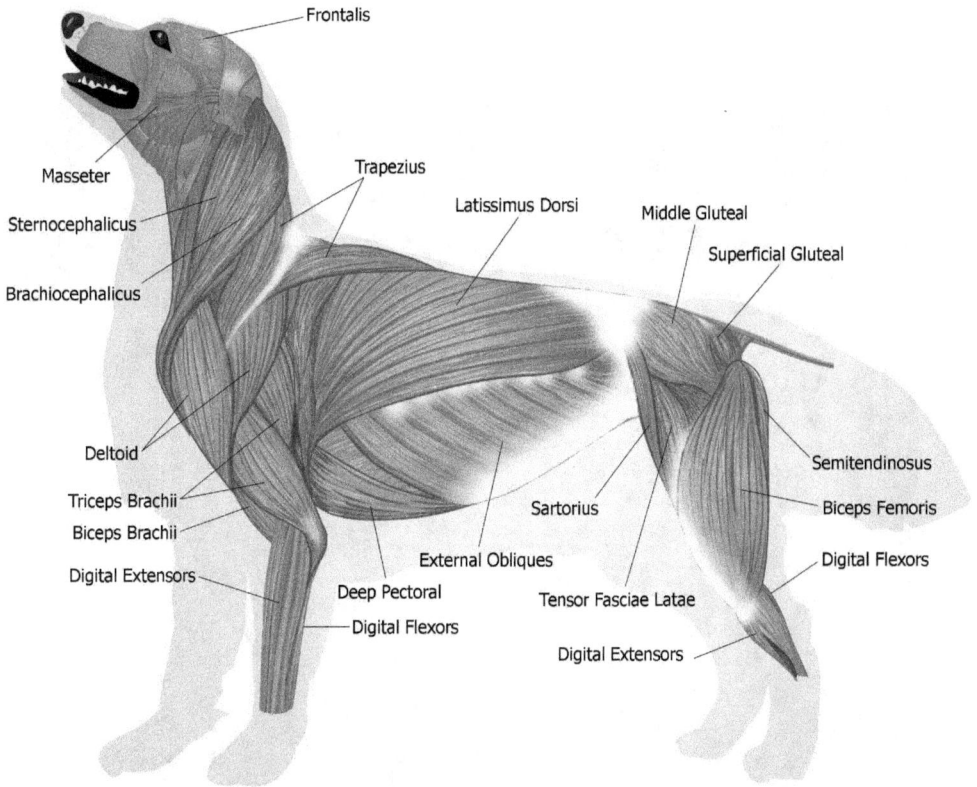

Canine Superficial Muscles —Side View

Muscles keep the body moving and working. Voluntary muscles are muscles controlled by thought. Skeletal muscles fall into this category; they are responsible for the dog's movement. Involuntary muscles continue to work without thought. Stomach muscles, cardiac muscles, and respiratory muscles fall into this category. It is the voluntary muscles that are worked during a massage session.

CHAPTER FIVE
Effleurage Massage Technique

This chapter explores the details and variations of effleurage massage. The effleurage stroke can range from a soothing, relaxing stroke that is light and comforting to one that involves finger, thumb, or whole hand pressure working to move fluids, release toxins, and aid in muscle relaxation.

What is the Technique?

There are two basic techniques for performing effleurage: one-handed and two-handed. Whether you're using one hand or two hands, the hand technique is the same:

- keep your fingers together as you stroke your dog,

- use even pressure throughout the stroke,

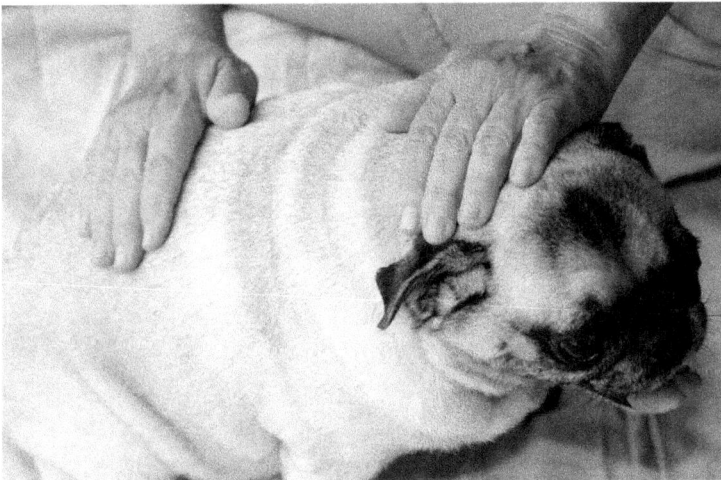

- repeat the stroke several times over the same area of the body,

- move smoothly between one body part and the next, and;

- maintain contact at all times with at least one hand.

In most cases, effleurage strokes follow the direction of your dog's fur. On the inside legs however, the stroke should go against the fur, toward the heart. This helps with circulation by assisting blood flow returning to the heart.

Stroke frequency should be a minimum of three to five times per area of the body before moving on to other areas of the body. The stroke pressure and rate varies depending on your intent.

- Slow rates, such as one stroke every two or three seconds with light pressure can be calming and aid circulation.

- Slow rates with firm pressure increases blood and lymph circulation and is used to drain fluids and toxins from larger areas of the body.

- Faster rates of one or two strokes per second with light pressure can be stimulating and help with swelling or fluid retention.

- Faster stroke rates with heavier pressure can have a strong effect on circulation.

- Fast rates, more than two strokes per second, energizes your dog and is effective as a pre-event warm up or before exercise.

One-Handed Effleurage

One-handed effleurage is often mistaken for simple petting. After all, the technique looks similar to petting your dog, however, there are differences. When performing one-handed effleurage, your focus is on healing the area of the body you are massaging. Use one hand only to stroke a specific body part, while leaving the other hand in a stationary position on your dog's body. Your stroke should be smooth, rhythmical, and even in pressure.

With one-handed effleurage, your options are to use your entire hand, one or more of your fingers, or your thumb. If you use your hand, use your entire hand to make contact with your dog during the stroke. If you are using two or more of your fingers, keep the fingers together and make full contact on the dog's body as shown on the next page.

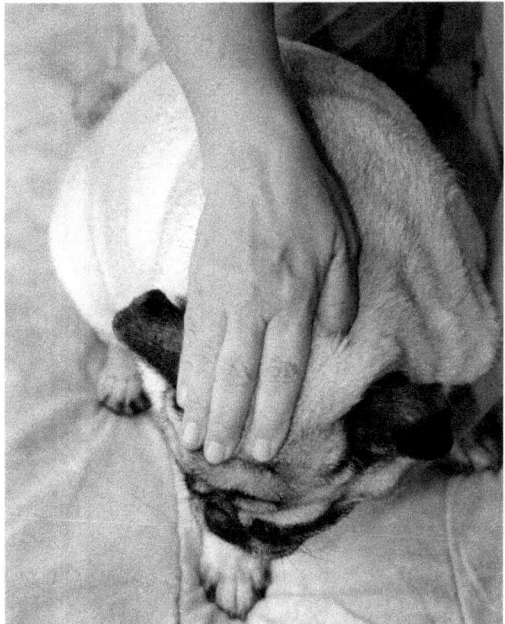

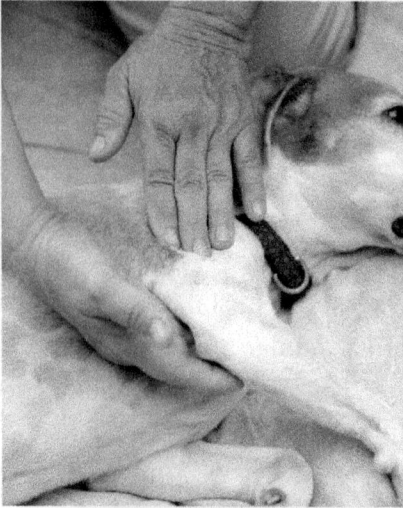

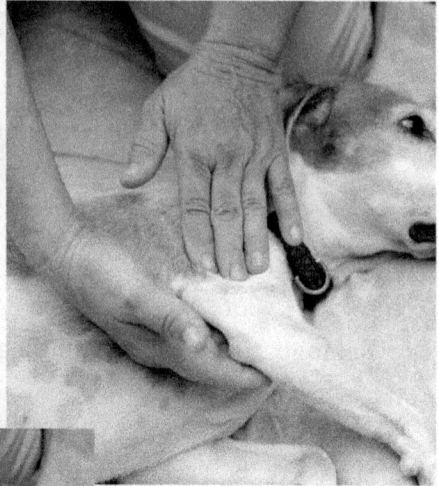

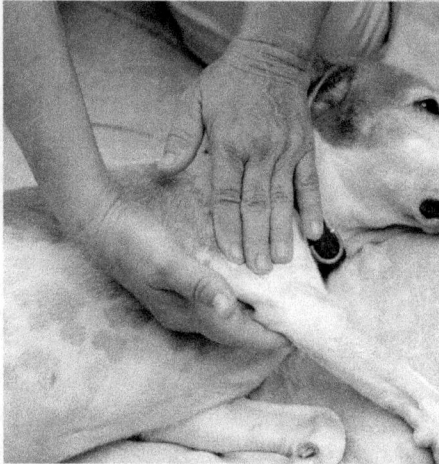

One-handed effleurage using three fingers along Bella's shoulder muscle, beginning at the top of the shoulder and moving down to the elbow, following the direction of the muscle and her fur. When I reach her elbow, I lift my right hand, move it back to the starting point at the top of the shoulder, and begin the stroke again. In this example, I'm using a heavier pressure and slower rate, which helps with circulation and drainage over larger parts of the body. Note her elbow is supported by my other hand. The effleurage stroke is repeated several times with one hand while the other hand remains stationary, supporting the elbow.

Two-Handed Effleurage

Two-handed effleurage is performed hand over hand, in a rhythmical manner. A stroke with one hand is followed by a stroke with the other hand over the same area, in a smooth, controlled, even-pressured and flowing manner. One hand makes contact with the dog's body at all times.

A variation on this stroke involves using both hands placed next to each other moving at the same time, in the same direction. At the end of the stroke, remove one hand, and place that hand at the stroke starting point, remove the other hand and place it at the stroke starting point, and repeat the stroke.

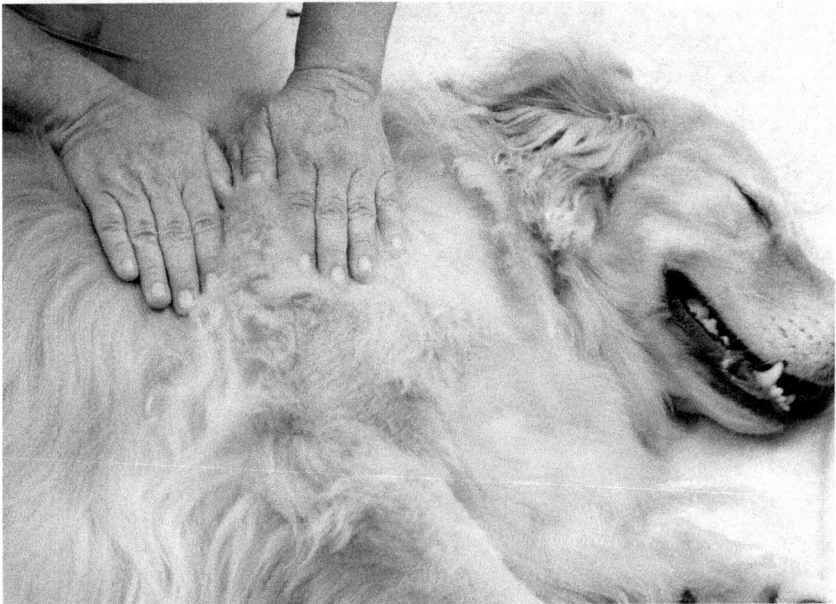

Your flat, relaxed hands should make full contact with your dog, and the stroke should follow the contours of your dog as you move through each individual stroke. Optionally on small dogs or smaller areas on a larger dog, instead of using your open hand, use the flat tips of the fingers or even your thumbs in the same manner.

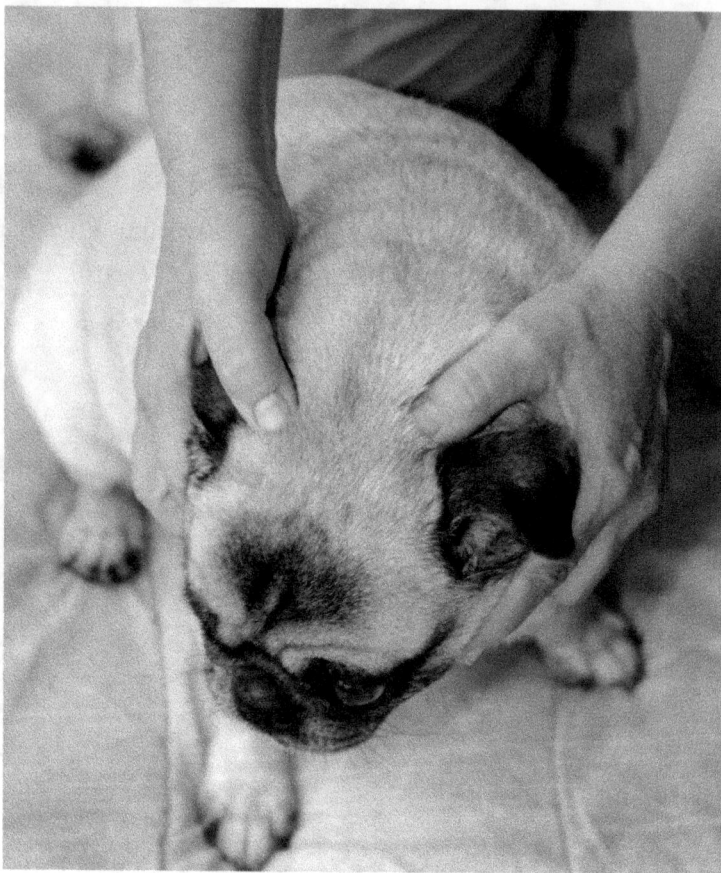

In the hand over hand stroke (illustrated on the next page), start the stroke with your first hand and when that hand is near the end of the stroke area, begin the next stroke with your other hand. When you are at the end of the stroke with your first hand, lift that hand completely off your dog's body and move the hand back to the starting point. Start a new stroke with this hand once the other hand nears the end of the stroke area. Repeat this cyclic movement with each hand, hand over hand.

Stroke duration is longer over larger parts of the body than smaller parts. For example, areas on either side of the spine should be treated as a long duration stroke, beginning at the neck area and ending at the tail, rather than breaking the stroke into separate smaller strokes covering the same area.

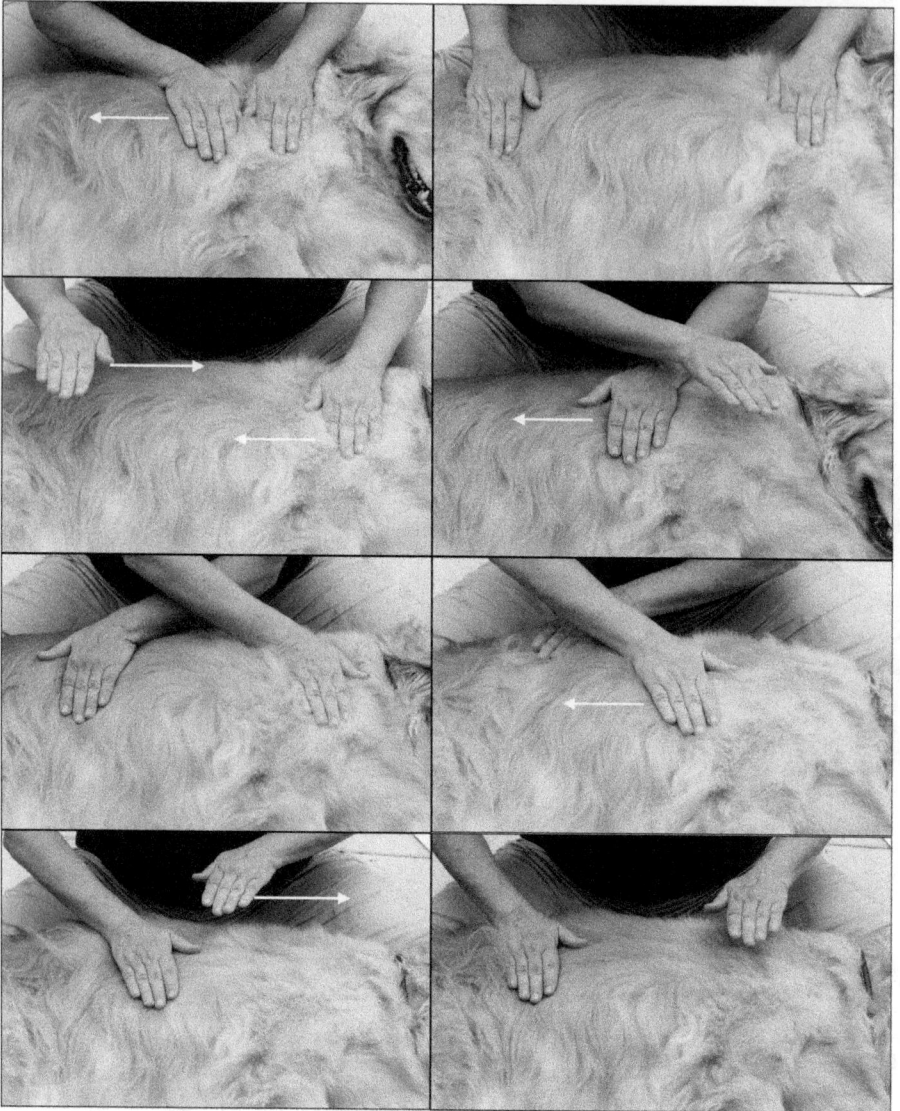

Begin each sequence with a full stroke with one hand, in this case my right hand. At the end of that stroke, I lift my right hand and begin to move it back to the starting position, while stroking with my left hand. As my right hand moves back to the starting position, my left hand completes the stroke. I then move my left hand back to the starting position beginning the sequence again with my right hand.

CHAPTER SIX
Variations in the Effleurage Stroke

Effleurage is a versatile stroke that provides varying effects depending on factors such as the speed of the stroke, the pressure, direction and hand placement. This chapter describes the application techniques that give this stroke such versatility. These techniques are pressure, frequency, direction, duration, rate, contact, and breath.

Pressure – describes the amount of force you apply with your hand or fingers to the area being massaged. This can range from feather light to heavy depending on the size of the dog, the amount of hair and muscle mass, the area being massaged, and the reason for the massage. Experiment on your arm or upper leg to get a feel for how much pressure you are using.

The following chart gives you a guideline for pressure ranges on each stroke:

Touch Type	Amount of Pressure
Finger Stroke (very light)	1 oz to 1/2 lb
Light of Delicate Touch	1/2 lb to 3 lbs
Regular or Mild Touch	3 to 5 lbs
Firm Touch	More than 5 lbs

Begin your massage with light pressure and work toward a heavier pressure as warranted. But make sure the pressure is not too light; feather light pressures can sometimes irritate the nerves beneath the skin.

If you are unsure of your approach, use a lighter pressure rather than a heavier one. Heavy pressures may not only hurt your dog, but can often cause damage such as muscle bruising. As you gain experience, you'll develop an intuition and get a feel for how much pressure you are using and how much is necessary to achieve the goal for the massage.

Frequency – the number of times you repeat a stroke per area of the dog's body before moving on to another area. Repeat each stroke a minimum of three times. As you gain experience, you will begin to know how many repetitions to use.

Direction – the path you use to move your hands across the dog's body, or the way in which you move his skin. This varies depending upon your objective. Most often, the direction your hand moves is the same direction the dog's fur or muscles lay. But, you can also direct strokes across the muscle fibers, or against the fur and toward the heart.

Duration – the amount of time you take to apply a single stroke. Certain areas of the body are better for long duration strokes, while other body areas may require shorter strokes.

Rate – the speed with which you apply your strokes. A slow rate is soothing and a great way to start your massage or move from one stroke area to the next. Slow strokes relax your dog, while faster strokes stimulate him. The rate may vary with each massage depending on the purpose of the massage, and may vary within a single massage session. As you gain confidence and experience, you will sense areas on your dog's body that that will benefit from either a slow or a fast rate effleurage stroke.

Contact – the way in which your hands make contact with the surface of the dog's body. There are several different techniques available depending on the size of the dog and the area you are massaging. You can:

- Use your whole hand flat against the dog. This is best used for bigger dogs on flat areas of the dog's body, such as along the spine or ribs, or the large muscles around the hips and thighs.

- Use your whole hand but at angles to the dog. Depending on the angle, the effect can be much more intense in the area you are working.

- Use a curved hand. This is used in areas where there is more contour, such as the legs.

- Use your fingers or your thumb. Be careful here to use the pads of your fingers or thumbs instead of the tip. On small dogs, you will use your fingers or thumbs much more than on a large dog.

Keep your hands flexible, and follow the contour of your dog's body. Maintain contact with at least one hand on the dog at all times during the massage to provide a feeling of continuity. Aim for weaving one massage area into the next, giving your massage a sense of flow. This will encourage your dog to relax.

Your own breath – an often overlooked component to a successful massage. Be aware of your own breath and time your breathing to the rhythm and rate of your massage strokes. This can help your dog become more aware of his own breath, and encourage him to breathe normally and relax.

Experiment with these techniques and find out what works best for you and your dog.

CHAPTER SEVEN
Using Effleurage on Your Dog's Body

Now that you've been introduced to the details of the effleurage stroke, it's time to look at the various parts of your dog's body and identify how best to use this massage stroke on these body parts.

The Head

Around your dog's head there are several areas that benefit from massage. These are:

1. Around the eyes.

Massage around the eyes using either your fingers or your thumbs, using light pressure and slow movement. Work your way around the entire eye, making sure you don't poke your fingers into the dog's eye sockets. Either massage one eye at a time, supporting your dog's chin with your other hand, or

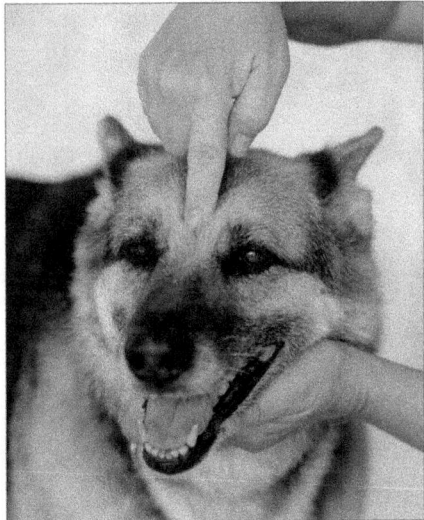

Rubbing between your dog's eyes affects an acupressure point that calms your dog.

37

position yourself so you can massage both eyes with your thumbs, while resting your fingers on the top of your dog's head. Massaging around the eyes can alleviate excessive tearing, itchy or dry eyes, sinus congestion, and other problems.

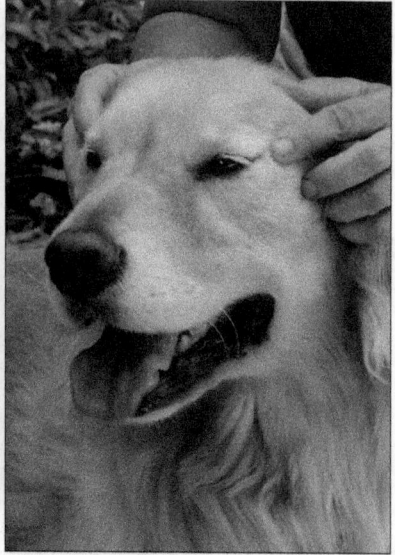

Use your fingers or your thumbs to gently stroke around your dog's eyes.

2. The jaw line, chin, and nose area.

From the outside of the eye slowly move down the cheek toward the jaw using your fingers or thumbs for effleurage strokes on and around the entire jaw line from the nose area to the masseter muscle; the muscle at the back of the jaw used in chewing. As with the eyes, use either one hand or both hands. When your dog is sitting or standing, you have the option of using both hands at the same time. Either massage with your thumbs while supporting your dog's chin with your fingers, or place your hands on either side of your dog's head and stroke from his nose toward the back of the head. Use a light effleurage stroke under the chin.

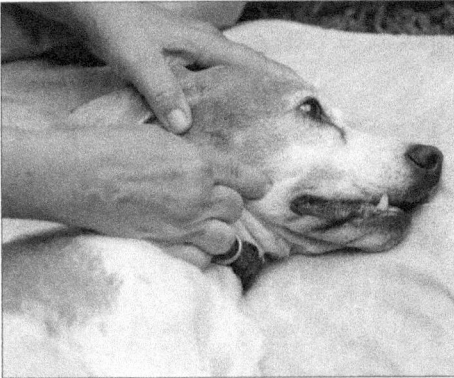

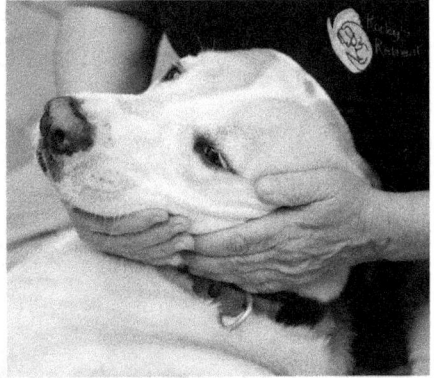

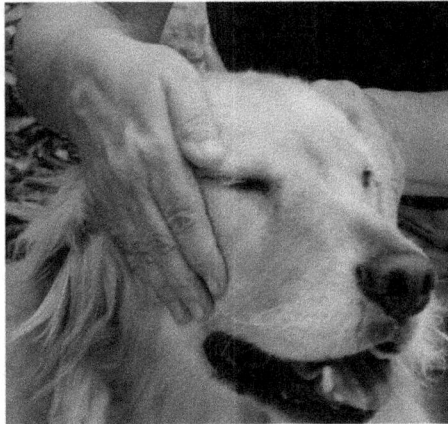

Clockwise from top left: effleurage on the masseter muscle at the jaw using a single finger, two-handed effleurage on the chin, and two-handed effleurage beginning at the nose, moving back toward the jaw.

39

3. The ears.

Start by holding your dog's ear with both hands near the base of the ear, and gently pull the ear out while using light pressure effleurage strokes moving from the base to the tips of the ears. Because there are many nerve endings in the ears, regular massage of the ears can calm your dog.

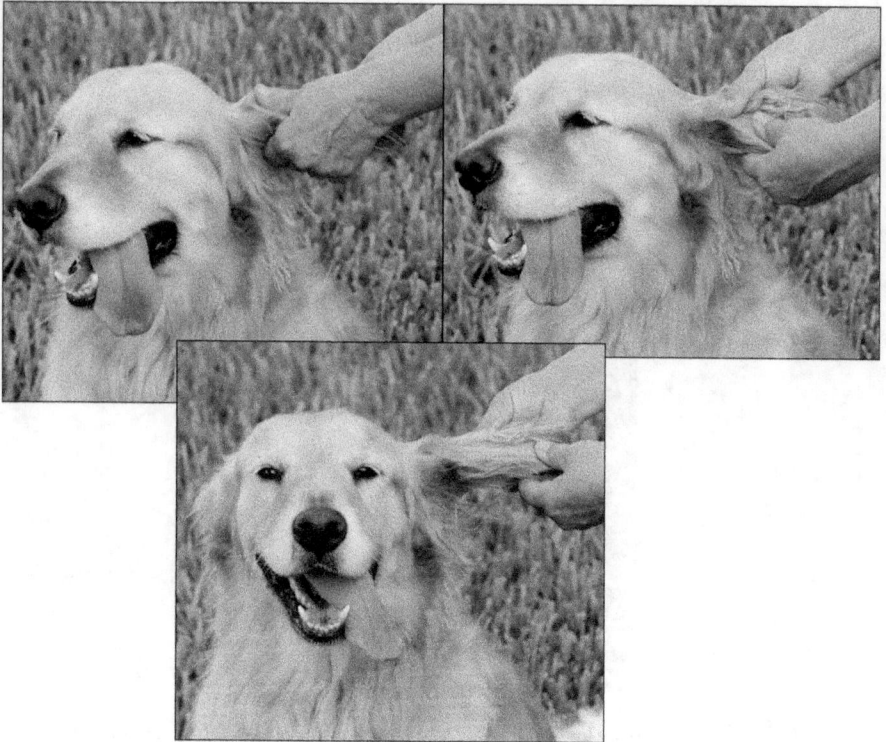

4. The top and back of the head.

Slow, gentle, light pressured effleurage strokes on your dog's head are an excellent way to calm him. This may seem like petting, and in a way it is; the difference is your intention, in this case, to give your dog a healing massage. Use one or two hands, but remember if you only use one hand, rest your other hand somewhere on your dog's body. Also use your fingers or thumbs to access the area on the head between and around the ears.

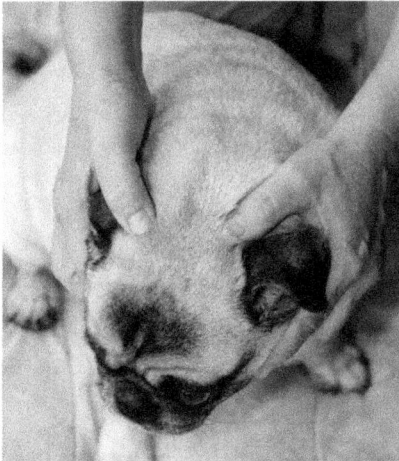

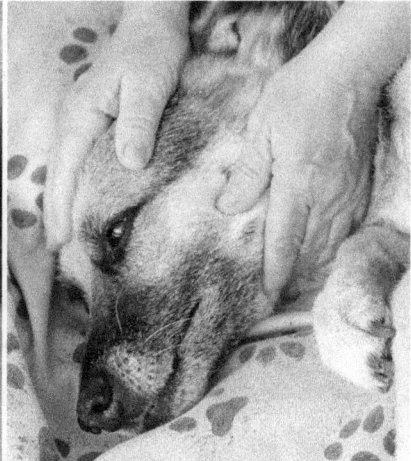

The Neck

Most dogs have a lot of skin around the neck area, which often lends itself to other massage strokes such as petrissage, or kneading, a stroke not covered in this book. However, effleurage can also work well on the neck muscles by using a firmer stroke. Massage all areas of the neck, including the sides, top and underside. Warm the area with light effleurage strokes prior to moving on to heavier pressure strokes.

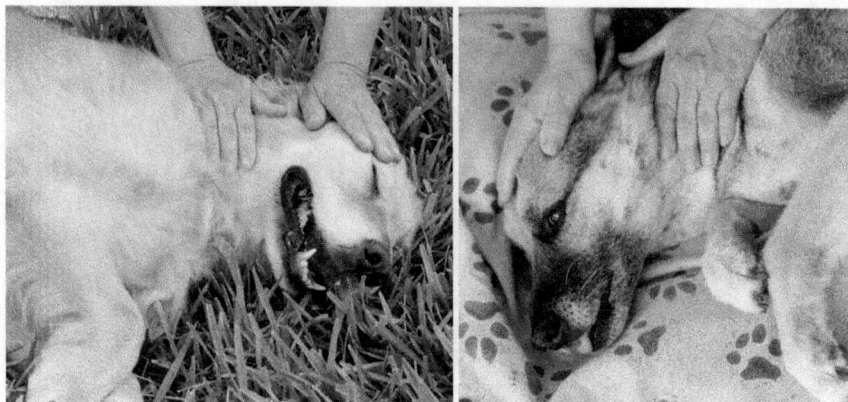

Withers and Shoulders

Because the withers and shoulders consist of larger muscles, you are able to use more pressure in your stroke. Warm the area using light, faster strokes and then work toward a slower stroke using deeper pressure. This is important if you feel adhesions (scar tissue), knots, or unusual tightness in this area. Shoulder muscles are vulnerable to adhesions and tightness, especially in active dogs.

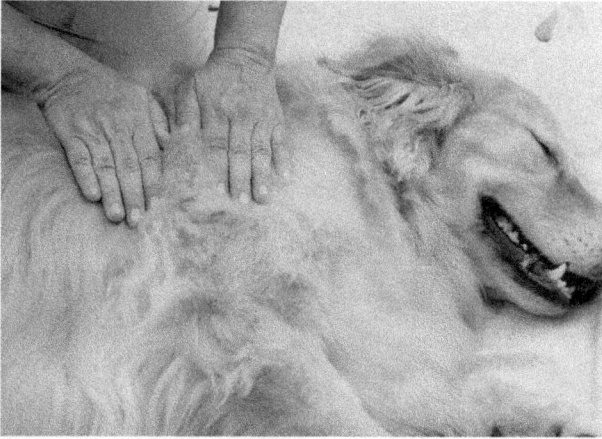

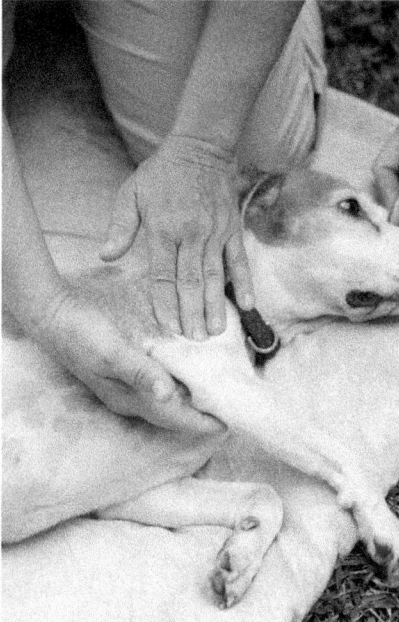

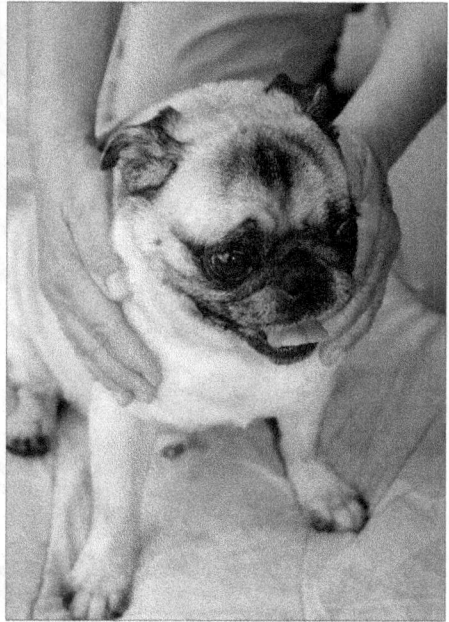

On the withers and shoulders, use your whole hand or use your fingers or thumb. With smaller dogs, use just your finger(s) or thumb. Use your fingers or thumb to isolate and work on an area where you feel adhesions, knots or tightness.

Chest and Abdomen

Gently lift your dog's front leg to work the chest and most important, the pectoral muscles. In most cases, a light effleurage stroke is most appropriate for the chest area. Use a heavier stroke on the pectoral muscles or on areas where you feel adhesions or some tightness. Light, fast strokes can improve respiratory or digestive issues.

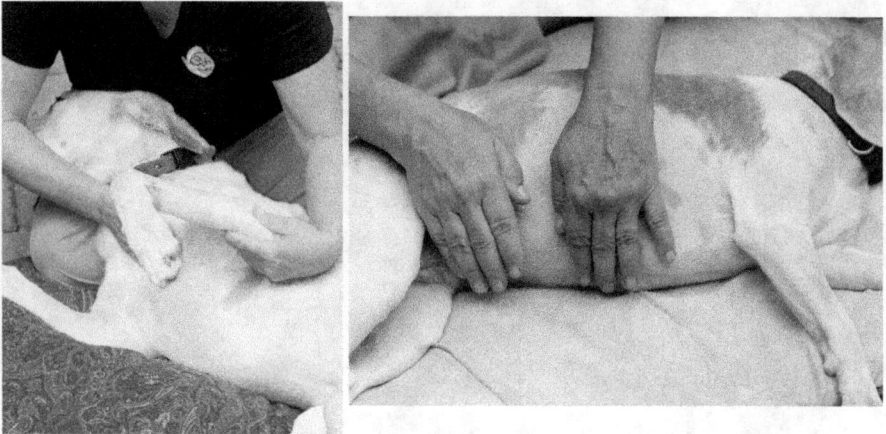

From left: lifting the leg to work the chest and pectoral area, two-handed effleurage on Bella's abdomen.

44

Back, Sacrum, Rib Cage, and Spine

Effleurage is a great stroke when used over this entire area to warm the long muscles predominant in this part of your dog's body. Use long flowing strokes along either side of the spine and down the rib cage. Spread your fingers when moving down the rib cage to access the muscles in between each rib.

Stroke pressure should be light. Stroke duration can be either slow or fast depending on your objective. Slow strokes are more calming and have a greater effect on muscles, circulation, and lymph fluid drainage, while fast, shorter strokes have more of an effect on the skin and nervous system. Effleurage here helps with spinal issues, back and hind-end problems, and skin and respiratory issues.

See examples on the next page.

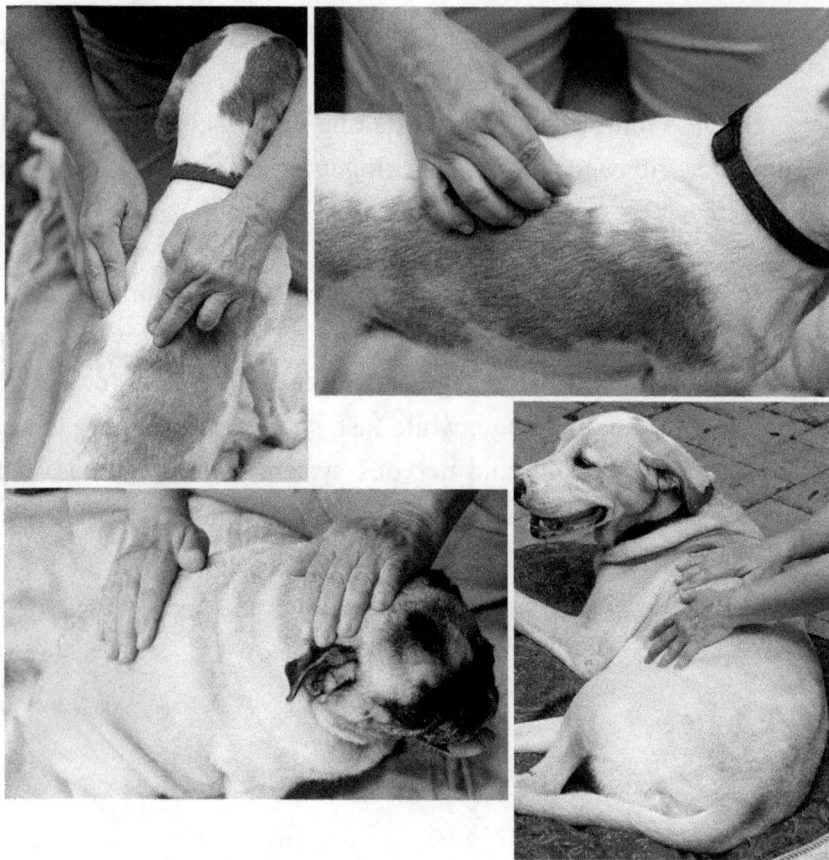

Clockwise from top left: two-fingered effleurage down either side of the spine, effleurage using fingers and thumb along the spine, two-handed effleurage along Gabe's rib cage, two-handed effleurage along Rascal's spine beginning at the top of the spine, moving to the sacrum.

Front Legs

Use a heavier pressure with your effleurage stroke in the muscled area on the upper part of the leg, between the shoulder and the elbow. Warm the area first using a lighter pressure stroke. Heavier pressure will loosen muscle tissues and bring blood flow to the area.

Use lighter pressure effleurage strokes in the direction toward the paws on the outside leg below the elbow. Follow this stroke with effleurage in the opposite direction from the paw back to where the leg meets the chest. This facilitates blood flow back to the heart and removes toxins from the body.

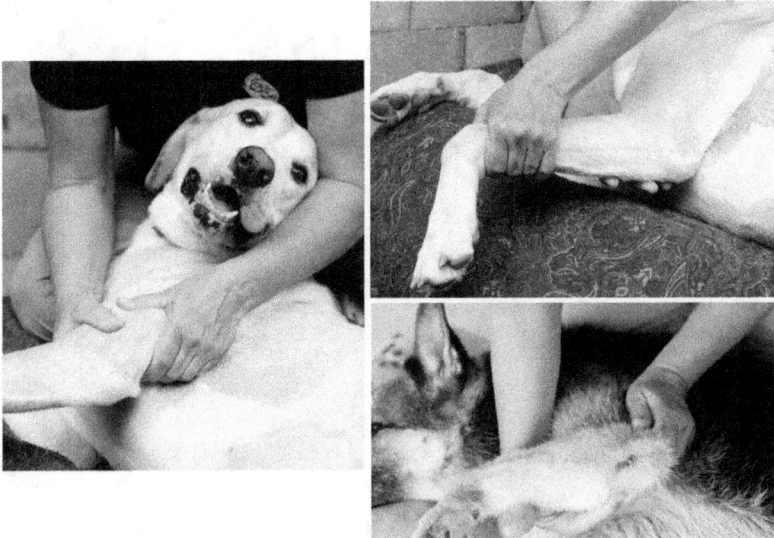

From left: effleurage using both hands wrapped around upper leg, one-handed effleurage wrapped around lower leg, flat one-handed effleurage on the inside leg, moving in the direction from paw to shoulder.

47

Hips, Thighs, and Back Legs

The most muscular part of the dog's body is the back-upper legs in the hip and thigh area with muscles such as the gluteals and hamstrings. These large, strong muscles are well suited to a heavier pressure effleurage stroke. Using a heavier pressure will get the circulation going and flush out toxins. Make sure the area is thoroughly warmed up with lighter, fast effleurage strokes prior to stroking with heavier pressure. Slow, deep pressure effleurage can break up adhesions or address muscle tightness that may be present.

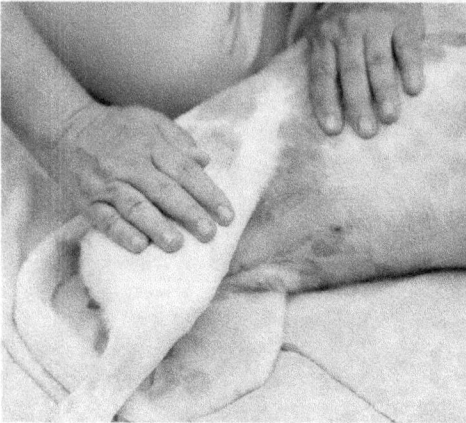

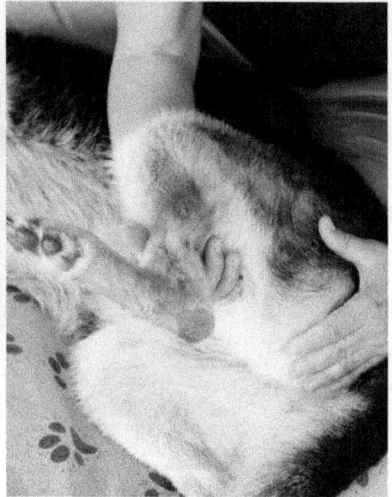

Left to right: one-handed effleurage on Bella's hip, effleurage on inside leg moving in the direction from paw to groin.

Just like the front leg, use lighter pressure effleurage strokes on the outside leg below the knee, moving in the direction toward the paw. Follow this stroke with effleurage in the opposite direction from the paw back to where the leg meets the groin area. Again, this facilitates blood flow back to the heart and removes toxins from the body.

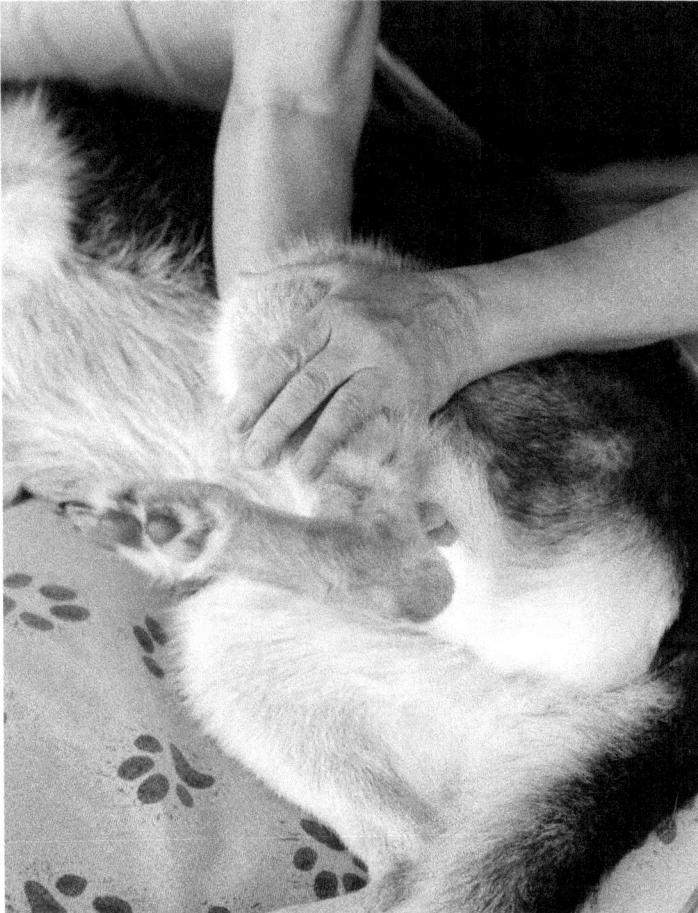

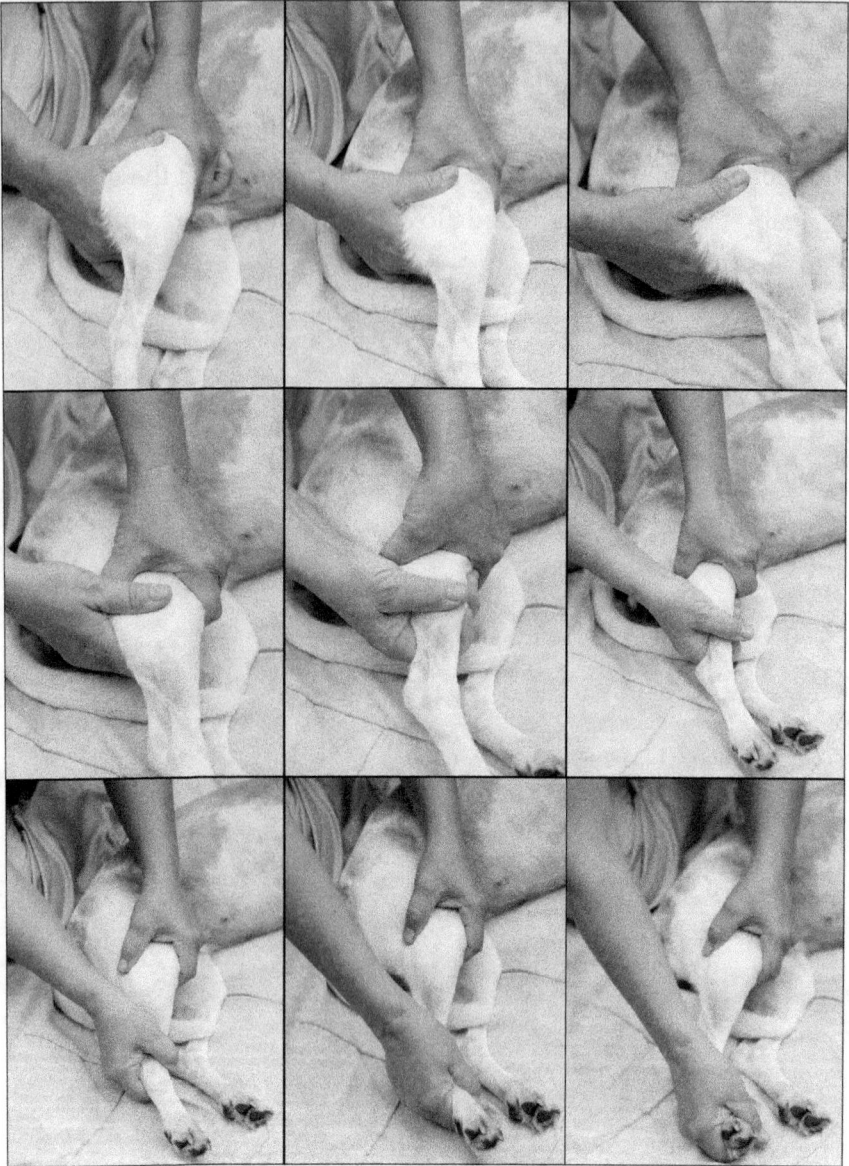

*Complete effleurage sequence on rear outer leg,
beginning with two hands on upper thigh, and ending
with one hand below the knee to the paw.*

Paws

The paws are sensitive areas for many dogs. If your dog is sensitive to his paws being touched, begin massaging them slowly. Start with very light, slow effleurage strokes, beginning at the wrist on the front leg or the hock (ankle) on the back leg. The main purpose with this stroke is to get your dog used to the idea you are touching with his paws. This is a great stroke to use on puppies. Once your dog is comfortable with his paws being touched, move to finger effleurage strokes using heavier pressure in and around his toes and the pads of his feet. This stroke is a good way to encourage blood flow to the paws and balance the energy throughout his body.

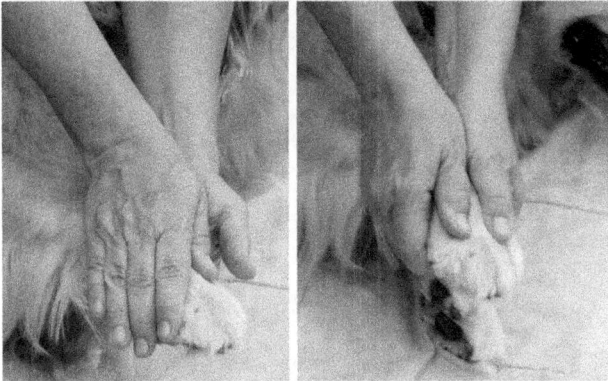

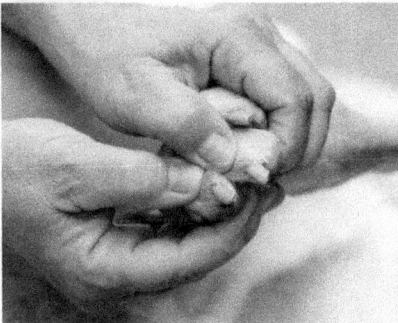

Clockwise from top left: effleurage on Miles' paw using my whole hand, using my thumbs, and heavier pressure effleurage on the toes.

51

Tail

Similar to a dog's paws, many dogs don't like their tails touched. If this describes your dog, massaging and stretching your dog's tail works well to overcome this dislike. One method is to circle both hands around the base of your dog's tail, keep one hand at the base and move the other hand toward the tip, using light effleurage strokes from the base of the tail to the tip of the tail. When the second hand reaches the tip, lift that hand and move it back to the base of the tail and repeat.

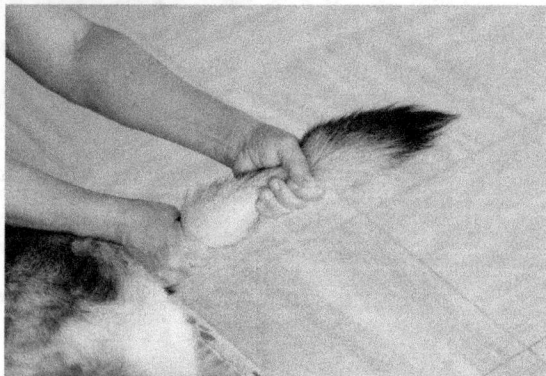

CHAPTER EIGHT
Guidelines for a Successful Massage

Massaging your dog should be a wonderful, relaxing and bonding experience, therefore, think about and prepare for the session using the following guidelines. *These guidelines are not all-inclusive by any means; they are suggestions to consider regarding the session.*

Setting the Scene – Preparing for Your Dog's Massage

Pick a time and a place that suits you, your dog's needs, and the goal of the massage. You want your dog to be receptive to the massage. Both you and your dog must be ready. If you're stressed, find another time when you're relaxed. If your dog has a lot of pent up energy and needs some exercise, take him for a walk or give him some playtime and follow this activity with a massage. Here are examples of appropriate times that may work for you:

- Right after grooming.

- Before and/or after exercise, although you should wait at least an hour after strenuous exercise to do a full massage. A short post-event massage can be performed once your dog has thoroughly cooled after strenuous exercise. See chapter 10 for details on the post-event massage.

- Before bedtime.

- Any quiet time during the day, when both of you are relaxed.

Your dog needs to be receptive; it's up to you to determine what time of day works best for him. Dogs are like people, some are morning dogs, some are evening dogs, and some don't care. Work with your dog when he is most receptive and most willing to relax. The exception to this is if you are working on your dog either prior to or after exercise or an athletic or show event.

Fit your dog's massage into your daily or weekly routine. Schedule each session around the same time and/or same day for weekly massages. After a few sessions, your dog may ask for his massage by coming to you, leaning into you to get you to place your hands on parts of his body that feel good to him.

Additional Guidelines When Preparing for Your Dog's Massage

- Ensure your dog has no physical problems that would indicate a massage is unwise.

- Find a quiet location, away from the phone, other pets, and members of the household. Some dogs like soothing music; decide what music to play, if anything, as you become more experienced.

- Dogs have different temperature requirements. The temperature in the room you have selected should be suitable for your dog.

- Use soft lighting, instead of bright, glaring lights.

- If you have a big or medium sized dog, massaging him will be easiest if you are both on the floor. Put down a blanket or bedding if you think your dog would like that.

- If you have a small or medium sized dog, massage him on the floor, on your lap, or on a table, wherever you both are most comfortable.

- Wait at least two hours after your dog eats before giving a massage.

- Wear loose fitting comfortable clothing, remove excessive jewelry, and keep your nails short so you won't injure your dog.

- Create enough space so your dog can get up and move around if he desires.

- Set your intention to that of healing your dog. Tell yourself you are healing your dog.

- Ask for permission to massage your dog. You don't have to say this out loud, just think the question.

During the Massage

- Your dog can be standing, sitting or lying on his side, depending on what is comfortable for him. Your position (sitting on the floor, on a stool, a chair or standing) will depend upon his position. You should be able to reach his entire body without straining.

- If you are on the floor or a chair/couch with your dog, sit in a comfortable position and center yourself. Maintain good posture throughout the massage session. If your dog is lying down, you should face his back, instead of his legs, to prevent yourself from possibly being kicked.

- If you are standing, maintain a straight back with no shoulder tension.

- Talk to your dog in a soft and soothing tone and praise him for being such a great dog.

- Breathe deep and slow to keep yourself relaxed and focused.

- Start with a light pressure and work to a deeper pressure as warranted.

- Take your time. If you don't have the time or are not in the mood, don't massage your dog. The massage session should be a pleasant experience for both of you.

- Note anything you feel or sense during the massage, such as knots, tightness, and areas of heat or cold. Notice your dog's reactions to the massage.

- Your dog may get up and shake, stretch, or get a drink of water during the massage. Let him. It's perfectly normal.

- If your dog doesn't want to be massaged, stop and try again another day. At first, some dogs because of the breed or past history may not like being massaged. However, with time, your continued practice, and patience, your dog will learn to love his massage.

> *It is important to maintain good posture while you are working on your dog. When you do, you will avoid fatigue, ground yourself, and better connect with your dog. Your back should be straight but not stiff and your shoulders should be loose but not hunched over. Check your body for any tension and release it. Relax your legs, especially if you are on the floor with your dog. Be aware of your breath, keep it relaxed, and try to time it with your strokes.*

CHAPTER NINE
Putting Together a Complete Session

Now, you are familiar with the effleurage stroke and have an idea how to use the stroke at different rates and pressures on the different parts of the dog's body. You also know the guidelines to prepare for the massage and to follow during the massage to ensure the most positive experience for you and your dog. Now let's look at the actual massage session. Where do you start? What are the stages of a complete massage session? How do you move from one area to the next without disrupting the flow of the massage? These are the questions answered in the next sections.

Stages of the Massage

In a full effleurage massage session, there are four stages – the opening, palpation, body, and the closing. The opening, body and closing are included in every massage you do on your dog. The palpation stage does not need to be included each time, but should be performed at regular intervals to ensure you notice changes in your dog's body.

1. **The Opening** – Set your intention, set the mood, and then ask your dog's permission. Begin to touch your dog using light strokes to quiet him, and encourage his relaxation. *This step should always be performed.*

2. **Palpation** – This is the assessment part of the massage. Run your hands slowly and gently over your dog's entire body to feel and assess his physical health. Make note of anything you feel is out of the ordinary. *This step does not need to be performed on every massage.*

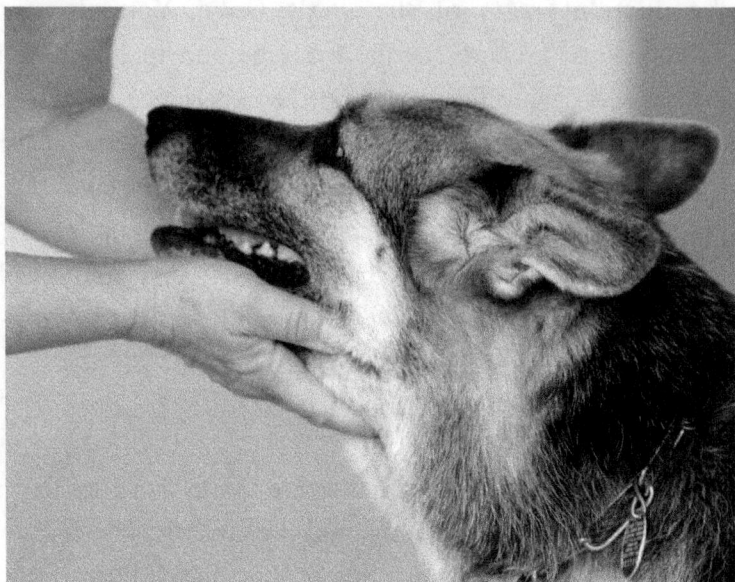

3. **Body** – The focus of the massage session. It's not necessary to do a full body massage every time. In each massage, decide how much or how little of a massage you want to do. Select the parts of the body to work, based on how your dog is feeling, what you want to address, your time limit, and other needs of the day. *This step should always be performed.*

4. **The Closing** – This important step is similar to the opening. In the closing, use light, slow, and gentle strokes over the entire body to reconnect and soothe all parts of the body, and ensure your dog is in a fully relaxed state. *This step should always be performed.*

The General Effleurage Massage Routine

This is a guideline to help you feel comfortable working on your dog. Once you gain experience massaging your dog, you won't need or want to follow a script like the one suggested below.

Create a smooth transition between areas being massaged to preserve the continuity, flow, and rhythm of the massage. This encourages maximum relaxation in your dog, whereas abrupt strokes, interruptions and unexpected changes make your dog tense, defeating the purpose of the massage. This may be a bit difficult at first, but with continued practice, it is a skill you'll master.

Most massages start at the head and end at the tail. Most dogs lie down on one side during the massage, which means you will work on one side of the body, ask your dog to turn over and then work the other side.

Opening the Massage.

- Find a quiet time when both you and your dog are receptive. Remove potential distractions.

- Set up mood particulars – music, lighting, candles, temperature, etc.

- Have your dog lie down in a place that is comfortable for both of you, be it on a couch (for smaller dogs), on his bed, or on the floor.

- Set your intention. Think about your dog being healthy and happy.

- Begin touching and stroking your dog using a slow and light pressure to soothe him, and encourage him to relax.

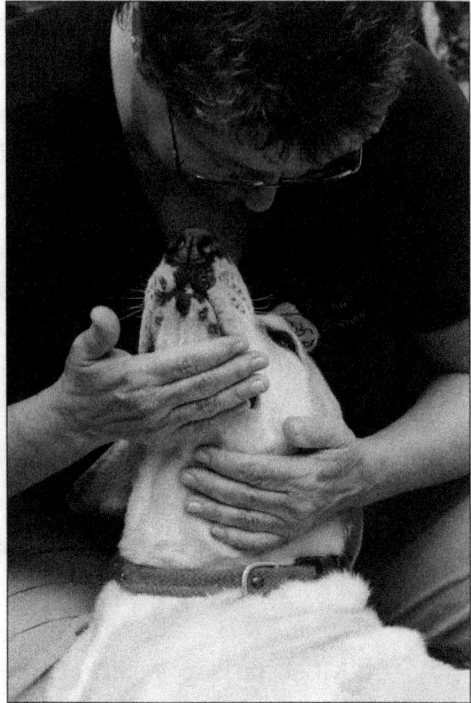

Palpation. If you choose to do this step, assess all parts of the body and note anything out of the ordinary. Note areas that may be tender, hot or cold, tight or swollen. Also look for spots of abnormal hair growth or where you feel a slight depression. These should be addressed during the body of the massage.

The Body of the Massage. The main part of the massage where most of the work is done. The steps that follow assume your dog is lying down on his side and describe work done on one side of the body. For consistency, massage both sides of the body. If your dog is small, turn him over yourself, but if your dog is large, it's better to ask him to get up and turn over. Forcing a dog to turn over may cause injury.

> *During a session, dogs will often yawn, lick their lips, get up and "shake it off", go get a drink of water, etc. If this happens during your dog's massage, let him do what he needs to do. This is a sign he is enjoying the massage. Your dog will return when he's ready. If he doesn't return, consider the session over for the day!*

- Often you can work on your dog's head before he lies down. If so, massage the entire head, including the jaw, around the eyes, under the chin and top of the head, followed by the ears.

- If your dog is already lying down, massage the one side of the head, including the ear. End the head massage with effleurage strokes flowing into the neck.

- Massage the neck area with light effleurage to warm the area and then move on to either a faster rate or heavier pressure to encourage blood flow to the area.

- With light strokes, move from the neck to the shoulder. Once the shoulder is warmed up, use heavier pressure to bring blood to the area. Give special attention to any adhesions or areas that feel tight.

- Gently lift the front leg and begin to use small effleurage strokes to open the pectoral region of the chest to prepare it to be massaged with the rest of the leg.

- Continue on to the rest of the front leg, while leaving the shoulder open. Stroke the entire leg, both inside and outside, including the shoulder and chest with effleurage strokes. Stroke from the paw to the elbow or shoulder to aid blood flow returning to the heart.

- Gently massage the paws on top, in between the tips of the toes and in between the pads if your dog will allow the work on his paws.

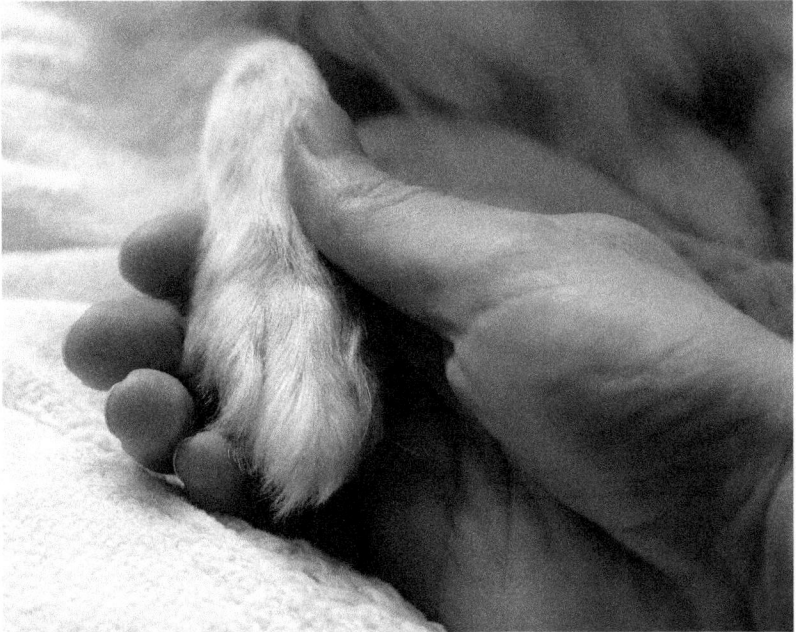

- Close the entire shoulder, pectoral area of the chest and leg, and moving on to the spine, rib cage, and abdominal region.

- Use light pressure effleurage strokes along the spine, down the ribs and onto the abdomen.

- Next, move on to the hips and back legs. Take time to warm the large thigh muscles thoroughly.

- Stroke the entire leg, both inside and outside, including the hip area with effleurage strokes. Use both hands to wrap around the leg at the upper leg, to cover both inside and outside at the same time, as you move your hands toward the paw. Finish stroking from the paw to the knee or up to the groin area to assist blood returning to the heart. Close the hip and leg area with some light pressure effleurage strokes over the entire area.

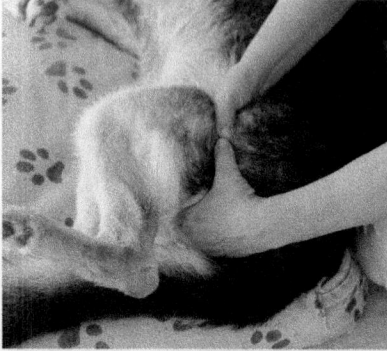

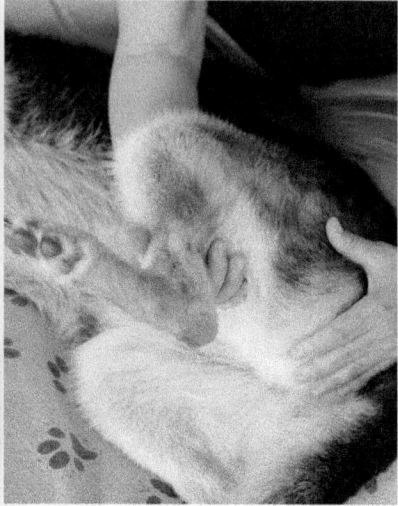

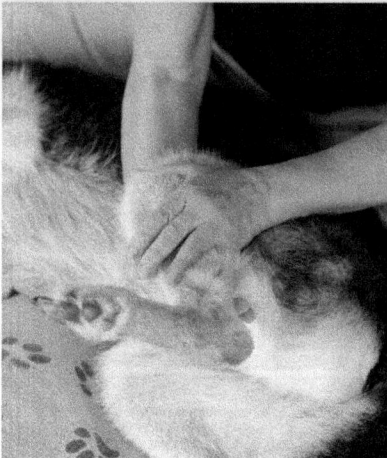

As shown: wrap your hands around the leg and move toward the paw, then stroke from the paw to the groin area.

- Follow the same procedure for the rear paws as you did for the front paws, only doing as much as your dog allows.

- Spend a moment or two on the tail if your dog will allow it.

The Closing.

- Use slow, smooth, light effleurage strokes all over your dog's body, beginning at his head, and ending at his tail, to connect all parts of the body and to complete his relaxation. If your dog is lying down, perform this sequence on one side at a time. Work on one side, close the side; work on the other side, then close that side.

- Finish your session with three long, smooth strokes beginning at the dog's head and moving to the tip of the tail along the either side of the spine (six strokes total). This final stroke set is a great way to balance energy throughout the dog's body.

- Give your dog a big hug and thank him for allowing you to have this incredible experience with him!

CHAPTER TEN
Considerations for Older or Working Dogs

Massage is important for all dogs, particularly for elderly or working dogs. For different reasons, we, as dog lovers and owners, need to help both our senior and working dogs stay as fit as possible. We need to keep blood flowing at optimum levels through the body, while flushing toxins from the body. We need to address issues of flexibility by working on adhesions and areas of tightness. The health of elderly or working dogs can be enhanced through regular effleurage massage.

Older Dogs

With older dogs, effleurage massage can keep your dog flexible, ease the pain of arthritis and other conditions, and keep blood, fluids, and joints moving in dogs that have problems in their ability to get up and go. Effleurage is a good technique to use on elderly dogs because it can be such a gentle and easy stroke.

If your older dog is new to massage, take your time and start with slow, short sessions. Effleurage is a great way to get your dog used to massage, while also working to get blood and energy moving. Be careful with your strokes on your senior dog; never use a heavy pressure. Instead, choose a lighter pressure to be safe, particularly around bony areas. Vary the speed of your effleurage stroke to move fluids through the body and facilitate toxin removal. Work on areas that feel tight to maintain your dog's flexibility. Through regular effleurage massage, you address common issues found in older dogs; arthritis, muscle atrophy, toxin buildup, circulation problems, immune system compromise, and more.

Working Dogs

On the other end of the physical spectrum from senior dogs are working dogs. Working dog categories include assistance dogs, detection, search and rescue dogs, show dogs, and performance athletes. The needs in a massage for this type of dog are different than most other dogs.

While successful working dogs love and live for what they do, they nonetheless experience a great deal of stress associated with their "profession." The stress can be mental, physical or both. Regular massage works to relieve stress, aids relaxation, and helps working dogs keep their focus when on the "job."

By giving effleurage massages on a regular basis, you help your working dog stay relaxed and in top physical and mental shape. Pre-work warm up and post-work cool down massages are also of benefit to prevent injury, remove toxin buildup, and maintain overall fitness and mental clarity.

Canine Athletes

Canine sports massage is an area within the massage field that involves warm up, cool down and other massage techniques that are geared toward the canine performance athlete. The subject is a topic beyond the scope of this book. If you have a dog that is a serious competitor or skilled athlete, seek out a qualified sports massage practitioner to keep your dog in peak physical and mental condition.

However, if you have a dog that participates in organized events as an amateur and you would like to try some basic warm-up and cool-down techniques with your dog, here is some general information.

Before exercise or competition.

- The intent of a pre-event massage is to increase circulation, thoroughly warm and lengthen muscles, and increase flexibility.

- Use light but fast paced effleurage strokes over the majority of the body.

- Perform the massage about an hour before exercise, and don't massage for longer than 10 to 15 minutes.

- Keep your dog warmed up until the event; don't allow him to lie down and cool down.

After the exercise or competition.

- The intent of a post-event massage is to rid the body of toxins that build up during intense exercise, help your dog relax, soothe muscles, speed recovery, and to notice areas of possible concern such as injury, swelling, or tenderness that may occur as a result of the event.

- Walk your dog after the event to make sure he has fully cooled down prior to performing a cool-down massage.

- Perform the closing sequence described in chapter 9. The purpose is to provide a short 10 to 15 minute relaxation massage over his entire body.

In between events. Perform effleurage massage on your dog at regular intervals, at least weekly, to keep him in top physical condition.

Fun Time with Your Dog!

You now have an excellent and easy to learn tool to perform effective and enjoyable massages on your dog! Now, comes time to practice. I can assure you with continued practice, you will not only become proficient, but you will create a lasting and loving bond between you and your dog. However, if you ever have doubts, review the material in this book, or schedule a session with a local qualified practitioner to learn what he/she does and apply the techniques to your own massage program.

Don't be afraid to ask questions, it's the best way to learn. Also, visit *www.healthydogsyourlovingtouch.com* or *www.OffTheLeashPress.com* to learn of new materials published on this subject.

Remember to ask your dog's permission and set your intention to give your dog a great massage. It is your intention and your focused effort on helping your dog that separates a massage from simple petting. If he doesn't want a massage, please honor his wish. Choose another time.

Allow your dog to enjoy the massage in the way that makes him most comfortable. If he chooses to get up in the middle of the massage, let him. If he only wants a short massage, end the session when he wants.

Keep in mind, you can decide how much or how little of a massage you want to perform in each session. If you are short on time but still want to massage your dog, focus your time on specific areas of your dog's body. If your dog has hip, joint problems, localized arthritis, or other conditions concentrate on those areas of discomfort or concern with shorter, more frequent sessions.

Choose a time when you are emotionally and energetically available to give your dog a massage. This should be a pleasurable experience for you and a way of increasing the bond with your dog, and this won't happen if you are stressed from the day's activities, if you are worried, tired or whatever.

Massaging your dog is a great way to get to know your dog on a different level. And, by giving the gift of massage, you are rewarding your dog for a lifetime of companionship and friendship. Good luck and most important - have fun!

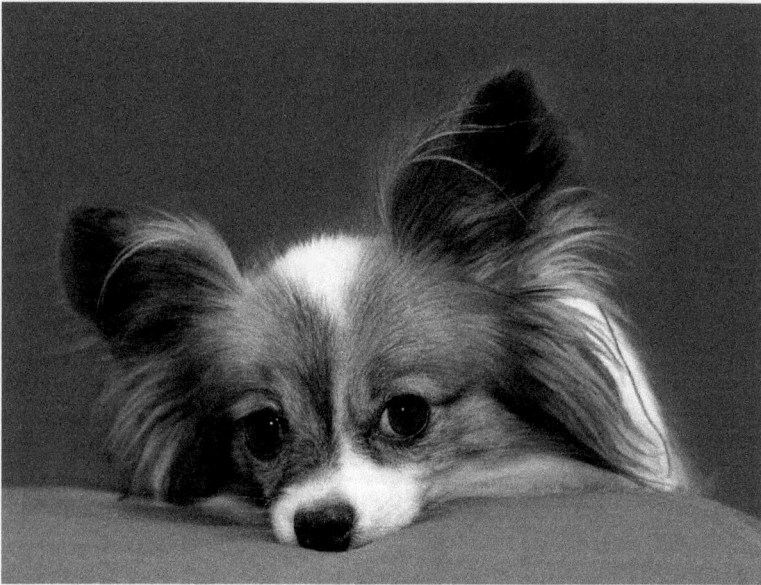

Glossary

Adhesion – A band of scar-like tissue that forms between two separate tissues that are not connected to each other. Adhesions are often caused by inflammation, surgery, or injury.

Assessment – The process of making an evaluation, a preliminary examination with the goal of ascertaining overall health.

Atrophy – A breakdown of tissues; a partial or complete loss of muscle mass and strength, due to prolonged immobility, aging, or diseases such as cancer.

Contact – The way in which your hands make contact with the surface of the dog's body.

Direction – The way you move your hands across the dog's body. Most often this will be in the direction of the dog's fur.

Duration – The amount of time you take to apply a single stroke.

Effleurage – A versatile, gliding massage stroke that follows the contours of the body, encourages relaxation, warms the body, improves focus and mental acuity, increases circulation, and works to remove toxins and fluids from the body.

Frequency – The number of times you repeat a stroke per area of the body before moving on to another area.

Hock – The ankle joint on a dog, located on rear leg, below the knee.

Inflammation – One way the body reacts to harmful stimuli, such as infection, irritation, or injury, in an attempt to protect the body. Inflammation is characterized by redness, swelling, heat, and pain.

Integrated therapies – A combination of conventional and alternative medical treatments with the emphasis on prevention. Massage falls into the category of integrated therapies.

Lymph (lymph fluids) – Fluid circulating throughout the body to nourish the cells, and collect and eliminate toxins.

Massage – The manipulation of skin, muscles, and joints for the purpose of affecting physical or emotional changes in the body.

Masseter muscle – The muscle at the back of the jaw that is used in chewing.

Palpation – A method of assessing the body during a physical exam using your hands to note structural landmarks, determine general health, and feel for anything out of the ordinary.

Pectoral – A thick muscle located on the upper part of the chest.

Petrissage – A group of massage strokes that apply pressure through movements that knead, press, squeeze, lift, roll, or wring the muscle tissues with the goal of improving circulation, removing waste and encouraging relaxation.

Pressure – Describes the amount of force you apply with your hand or your fingers to the area being massaged.

Rate – The speed with which you apply your massage strokes.

Sacrum – The large triangular shaped bone at the base of the spine.

Scapula – The shoulder blade.

Stifle – The dog's knee, located on the hind legs.

Toxin – A poisonous substance produced by living cells or organisms.

Withers – The ridge between the shoulder blades on four-legged animals. On dogs, the withers is the standard place to measure the dog's height.

About the Author

Sherri Cappabianca is certified in small animal massage through Northwest School of Animal Massage. She received her initial certification in September 2006, and since then she has continued to study massage through Northwest, completing subsequent certifications. She is certified in small animal acupressure through Tallgrass Animal Acupressure Institute, aromatherapy from the School of Essential Balance,

Sherri and Yankee

and is also a 6th generation Reiki Master in the direct lineage of Usui, Hayashi, Takata, Gray and Rosenthal.

A former software engineer with a BS in Computer Science, Sherri decided to pursue canine massage after she had a vivid dream about canine massage. After working in telecommunications for many years, she wanted a career change out of the software field. A life long dog lover, she acted on the dream, began her studies, and in 2006 opened her canine health

79

and wellness business, Rocky's Retreat, named after the special canine soul who inspired her on this path.

Since then, Sherri has been helping dogs and their "parents" throughout the central Florida area. She wrote her first book *"Healthy Dogs, Your Loving Touch: Acupressure Massage for Your Dog"* because of her passion for teaching people how to massage their own dogs. In doing so, she believes she can help that many more dogs live healthier and happier lives.

Sherri lives in Winter Park, FL, with her husband Pasquale and their dog Yankee.

Rocky, at one of his favorite places,
Captiva Island, in southwest Florida.

To learn more about Sherri, her books, or other products offered through Off The Leash Press, LLC, please visit *www.OffTheLeashPress.com*.

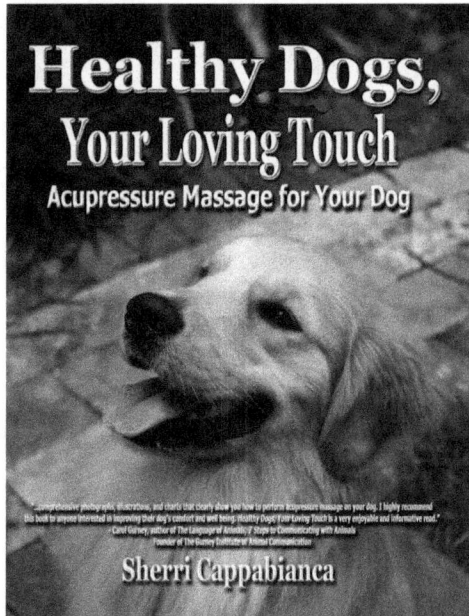

Sherri's first book "Healthy Dogs, Your Loving Touch: Acupressure Massage for Your Dog."

www.OffTheLeashPress.com